The Property Tax Handbook for Investors

Copyright © 2021 by JSM Success Ltd

All rights reserved. This book or any portion thereof may not be reproduced or used in any manner whatsoever without the express written permission of the publisher except for the use of brief quotations in a book review.

First published March 2021 in The United Kingdom. For more information, please visit our website at www.jsmpartners.co.uk

Get in Touch
Email: joshua@jsmpartners.co.uk

JSM
Brightfield Business Hub
Bakewell Road
Peterborough
PE2 6XU

ISBN: 9798726987392
Imprint: Independently published

The Property Tax Handbook for BRRR & BTL Investors

This publication is produced for general guidance only and professional advice should be always be sought. Nothing contained within this publication constitutes accountancy, tax, investment, legal, or other professional advice.

JSM Success Ltd and the author make no warranties or representations as to the correctness or completeness of this publication and as such, we do not accept any liability or responsibility for any loss, of any nature, whether direct or indirect, which may arise from reliance on this publication.

The practices of the Government and other regulatory bodies, namely **HM Revenue and Customs**, are often subject to change, as are the tax legislation and wider legal environment. The focus of guide is towards **UK** resident taxpayers, however regional variations do exist and are not included within this guide. For this reason, you should always consult a suitably qualified professional adviser when requiring professional advice. Any examples contained within this publication are based on several assumptions and generalisations, not all of which will be contained within the body of text. Rates and figures quoted can be assumed to be for the 2021/22 tax year unless otherwise stated.

Your personal circumstances will vary from any examples contained within this publication, as such any outcome or result may not be applicable to your personal circumstances. Your professional adviser will be able to determine whether any reliefs, benefits, or outcomes are applicable to your personal circumstances, taking into consideration all and any relevant factors. Any persons contained within the examples are completely fictional and are not based on any actual persons, either alive or deceased.

The Property Tax Handbook for BRRR & BTL Investors

Contents

Introduction... 1

What taxes do property investors pay?...................... 4

What type of property investor are you?................... 36

How to structure your property business?.................. 43

Setting up your limited company........................... 56

What taxes apply when buying property?.................. 78

Running a limited company............................. 93

Profit extraction from a limited company..............114

My favourite tax deductions............................ 126

FAQs...131

The Property Tax Handbook for BRRR & BTL Investors

Introduction

As one of the leading property specialist accountant's in the sector I have the pleasure of working with hundreds of property investors, meaning I see first-hand what makes the difference between amateur property investors who barely break-even and the titans of the sector who own multiple houses in multiple streets, collecting tens of thousands a month in rental profits.

In my opinion one of the biggest factors is that the professional landlords and investors treat it as a full-time business, being completely aware of all costs, what money is coming out, when it's going out, a complete financial understanding.

Believe it or not the biggest expense in a property investment business is often the tax bill and as a result those who seek proper professional advice reap the benefits with increased cash going straight into their bottom line.

Therefore, developing an understanding of the tax system is an absolute must for any property investor who really wants to grow and scale a profitable, cash-rich, property investment business. I am not saying that you need to complete your Chartered Tax Advisor qualification and become an expert, you just need to make a conscious effort to invest in your financial education so that you can fully understand what your accountant is talking about and hold them to task when you feel they're not doing their job.

Books and other resources on tax are notoriously long, complicated, and difficult to digest with most books on the subject being written for accountants and lawyers, with page counts running in the high hundreds if not thousands. It's for this very reason I have distilled the key areas of property tax that relate to **BRR and BTL** investors in this short and easy to follow book.

The Property Tax Handbook for BRRR & BTL Investors

The book is structured to go from the start to end in terms of the taxes you face as a property investor, this includes setting up your business structure and the tax issues there, how to calculate the Stamp Duty Land Tax liability when purchasing a property, and then some of the tax consequences when it comes to selling a property or the entire property business.

I would recommend skimming through the whole book and then homing in the areas you feel are most relevant to you depending what stage in your property journey you are.

The Property Tax Handbook for BRRR & BTL Investors

What Taxes Do Property Investors Pay?

Over the years property investors have faced a very hard time with a series of constant tax increases, first came the Section 24 mortgage interest changes which punished those who invested in their own names. Shortly following this was the 3% SDLT surcharge which made purchasing investment properties that bit more expense.

It's safe to say that as a property investor, tax can very much be seen as the enemy. Knowing your enemy is a must, therefore we will first start with an overview of the many different taxes that apply to a property investor in England. The taxes are similar in Scotland, Wales, and Ireland however for brevity the specifics have been omitted.

The Property Tax Handbook for BRRR & BTL Investors

Income Tax

Income tax was first introduced in 1799 by William Pitt the Younger in order to pay for weapons during the Napoleonic Wars, more than 200 years later it's still here and paid by most of us.

It's paid on various forms of income that we receive personally such as employment income from our jobs, trading profits of a business and also rental income from property and land.

Income tax is paid on a marginal basis, meaning each slice of income is taxed in the band in which it falls. For the 2021/22 tax year Income tax is charged as follows for employment, savings and rental income:

- First £12,570 of income is covered by the personal allowance meaning 0% tax rate.
- Next £37,700 of taxable income (this means after utilising your £12,570 personal allowance) is taxed at 20%.

The Property Tax Handbook for BRRR & BTL Investors

- Amounts from £37,700 to £150,000 are taxed at 40%, with amounts over £150,000 falling into the additional rate band subject to tax at 45%.

It's important to note that dividend income is currently taxed at lower rates to the income listed above.

- Where dividend income falls within the basic rate band, they will be charged to tax at 7.5%
- Where they fall into the higher rate band, they are taxed at 32.5%
- and dividends in the additional rate band are taxed at 38.1%.

Historically it was popular for a landlord to buy properties in their own name and let them out, this was because the Income tax treatment was favourable in that they could receive up to £50,270 in rental profits and pay less than 20% tax, even for the larger landlords paying tax at 40% on the profits that fall into their higher rate bracket was acceptable.

The Property Tax Handbook for BRRR & BTL Investors

However, as a result of the Section 24 mortgage interest restrictions that were introduced from April 2017 onwards the rules completely changed making it very inefficient from a tax perspective for most residential property landlords. We will cover these changes and the impact they have had for landlords in the later chapter covering different business structures.

As a property investor Income tax is pretty much unavoidable as it will apply to rental profits of an unincorporated landlord, the salary you take from your property limited company, and also the dividends you will take from your limited company.

Whilst unavoidable there definitely are ways to reduce it as much as possible, throughout this book there will be a host of tax saving tips and tactics that are guaranteed to save you Income tax.

The Property Tax Handbook for BRRR & BTL Investors

Important Reliefs and Exemptions

- Rent a room relief: Earn up to £7,500 a year tax free when letting a room in your home. More information available in HS223 on the HMRC website.

- Property income allowance: Individuals with property income of £1,000 or less need not file a return for this income or pay any tax on the profits. If you incur a loss it might be worth filing a return to ensure this loss is carried forward.

- Replacement of domestic items relief: This provides a deduction from taxable profits when replacing certain domestic items.

- Sideways loss relief: This enables a taxpayer to offset trading losses against other income or capital gains. This relief does not apply to losses from a property business.

The Property Tax Handbook for BRRR & BTL Investors

- Personal allowance: Income up to the personal allowance is free from income tax.

- Personal savings allowance: Basic rate taxpayers can receive £1,000 of interest income free of income tax per year, higher rate taxpayers can receive £500.

- Qualifying interest deduction: Where you take out a loan to invest in a partnership, or a company in which you own 5% or more of the share capital, you can claim relief against income tax for the amount of interest paid.

- EIS/SEIS income tax relief: If you subscribe to EIS/SEIS shares you may receive a 30%/50% deduction from income tax of the amount invested.

- Dividend allowance: Up to £2,000 of dividend can be received tax free each year.

National Insurance

National insurance applies to property investors in many different ways depending on the business structure you chose.

As an unincorporated landlord you may be liable to pay Class 2 National Insurance Contributions (NIC) where your property business constitutes a business in the eyes of HMRC. If your property business does not constitute a business, there is no requirement to pay any NIC.

We've taken the information here from one of HMRC's internal manuals (NIM23800) which provides some guidance on what constitutes a property business, and what does not.

A person who is liable to Income Tax on the profits arising from the receipt of property rental income will only be a self-employed earner for NICs purposes if the level of activities carried out amounts to running a business.

The Property Tax Handbook for BRRR & BTL Investors

The nature of property letting requires some activity to maintain the investment, but that is not enough to make it a business. For example, being a landlord normally involves:

- undertaking or arranging for external and internal repairs
- preparing the property between lets
- advertising for tenants and arranging tenancy agreements
- generally maintaining common areas in multi-occupancy properties; or
- collecting rents.

In order for a property owner to be a self-employed earner, their property management activities must extend beyond those generally associated with being a landlord (which include, but are not limited to, the above).

For example, ownership of multiple properties, actively looking to acquire further properties to let, and the letting of property being the property owner's main occupation could be pointers towards there being a business for NICs purposes.

A landlord will also be a self-employed earner if any of their activities amount to a trade for Income Tax purposes.

This could include, for example, receiving income from other services such as providing a bank of washing machines in a multi-occupancy block that is rented to tenants, or providing an ironing service to tenants. Running a guest house or hotel will also usually amount to a trade for Income Tax purposes, so an individual proprietor will be a self-employed earner for NICs purposes.

If a property owner has an agent who manages their property for them, things that the agent does should be attributed to the owner. 'Agent' includes a friend or family member, as well as a professional managing agent. However, a property owner will only be a self-employed earner on this basis if the things that the agent does for them (ignoring any other clients they might have) are enough to count as a business or trade.

Examples

Example one – Inherited Property
Samantha lets out a property that she inherited following the death of her great aunt. This will not constitute a business.

Example two – Full-time landlord

Bob owns ten properties which are let out to students. He works full time as a landlord and is continually seeking to increase the number of properties he owns for letting. Bob is running a business for NICs purposes.

Example three – Typical landlord duties

Claire owns multiple properties that are let.
She spends around half her working time carrying out duties as a landlord and is not looking to increase the number of properties she owns. If the only duties that Claire undertakes are those normally associated with

being a landlord, then this would not constitute a business.

Example four – Using a letting agent

Hasan purchases properties using "buy to let" mortgages. He places all letting duties in the hands of a property letting agent who acts as landlord on his behalf. If the only duties that the property letting agent undertakes for Hasan are those normally associated with being a landlord, then this would not constitute a business.

The rate of Class 2 NIC for the 2021/21 tax year is currently £3.05 per week, or £158.60 per year.

At current in order to qualify for the state pension you need to have a record of paying NIC, therefore if you do not otherwise pay any NIC or have gaps in your record, doing what is possible to result in your property activity being considered a business might be beneficial to ensure you get the maximum pension entitlement.

One thing to note is that where your profits from the property business do not exceed the £6,475 small profits threshold, you can claim an exemption from paying Class 2 NIC.

For property investors that are running their business through a limited company you will encounter NIC when taking funds from your company via a salary and PAYE. As your limited company is employing you there is the potential to be charged to NIC twice, once via Employers National Insurance Contributions and again as an employee.

We have gone into this in detail in the later section where we cover how to extract cash from your limited company.

The Property Tax Handbook for BRRR & BTL Investors

Capital Gains Tax (CGT)

When it comes to selling (or gifting) either your property or shares in your property company you will encounter Capital Gains Tax, the purpose of CGT is to tax the 'profit' arising from the uplift in the capital value of the asset being sold/gifted.

Tax Tip:

I thought it incredibly important to mentioned that CGT will usually be applicable when property is gifted as I see it on a daily basis where a mis-informed property investor is under the impression they can gift their property to their children, or sell at a reduced price of £1 and have no tax to pay.

In most cases where a transaction like this occurs HMRC will apply a market value rule, which results in the sale proceeds being swapped with the market value of the property being gifted, or sold at an undervalue. The impact here is that the taxpayer gifting the property may end up with a large CGT bill and no cash to pay it.

The Property Tax Handbook for BRRR & BTL Investors

Before undertaking any transaction like this, definitely get professional advice.

Each individual benefits from an Annual Exemption which results in the first £12,300 of capital gains in a year being tax free. Gains over and above this amount are taxed at a variety of rates depending on the type of asset being disposed of, and whether they fall into your basic or higher rate band.

The different rates are therefore:

- 0% where it falls within the first £12,300 annual exemption.

- 10% where the disposal qualifies for Business asset disposal relief (formerly entrepreneurs' relief). In practice this rarely applies to a property letting busines but does apply to Furnished Holiday Lettings and property trading businesses.

The Property Tax Handbook for BRRR & BTL Investors

- 10% on a disposal of non-residential property (shares and commercial property etc.) and the gain falls within the basic rate band.
- 20% on a disposal of non-residential property and the gain falls into the higher rate tax band.

- 18% on disposals of residential property where the gain falls into the taxpayers basic rate band.

- 28% on disposals of residential property where the gain falls into the higher rate band.

The rates above apply to individuals and partnerships. With regard to a limited company selling a property the gain is subject to Corporation Tax as explained in the section on exiting your property business.

I could easily write another book just on CGT but have had to cut out any form of detail to keep the book at a reasonable length.

The Property Tax Handbook for BRRR & BTL Investors

Important Reliefs and Exemptions

- Private residence relief: If you have previously lived in the property as your primary residence, then the gain accruing during this period will be tax free.

  - Lettings relief: If you let out a property you have previously lived in you can claim lettings relief. Since the most recent budget the conditions to be eligible for lettings relief have changed, meaning in the future it will rarely apply to landlords.

- Incorporation relief: Should the property business meet the criteria set out in case law, the property business can be transferred from an individual or partnership into a limited company with no immediate CGT liability.

- Gifts to spouses: Transfers between a married couple or civil partnership are not chargeable to CGT. Instead they acquire the asset at the original purchase price, meaning any gain made on the asset before the transfer will not be realised until a future disposal outside of the marriage.

The Property Tax Handbook for BRRR & BTL Investors

Corporation Tax

Property investors who invest via a limited company will pay corporation tax on their rental profits, the current rate for the 2020/21 tax year is 19%. There are no annual allowances or exemptions meaning if you've got £1 profit, Corporation Tax of 19p would be due.

From the start of the tax year 2023 onwards Corporation Tax is due to increase to a headline rate of 25%, however this will only apply to companies with large taxable profits. For companies with profits under £50k, the rate of tax will remain at 19%. For companies with profits between £50k-£250k the Corporation Tax rate will be tapered, increasing up to 25% as profits increase within this band.

Due to the Section 24 finance cost restrictions that were phased in from April 2017 a limited company has almost become the standard option for new property investors, this is mostly due to the ability to obtain tax relief in full on all mortgage and finance costs.

We'll cover Corporation Tax and how profits are calculated in the later section on running your property company.

Important Relief and Exemptions

- Loss relief: Companies that are in a 75% group can transfer losses for corporation tax purposes from one company to another. A 75% group is generally where a holding company owns at least 75% of the share capital of the two subsidiary companies, however a subsidiary company could also move a loss directly to a parent company.

Stamp Duty Land Tax

Where you purchase a residential property costing more than £40,000 which is not your first or primary residence Stamp Duty Land Tax (SDLT) will likely arise.

This means that for the majority of property investors purchasing property to let out there will be some SDLT to pay at the point of purchase.

Typically, your solicitor will handle your SDLT return and the payment of SDLT will be made at point of completion. The strict deadline for payment of SDLT is 14 days from the effective date of the transaction.

Where you are involved in a complex property deal where there might be semi-commercial elements it is important to obtain guidance from a SDLT expert as solicitors are not SDLT experts, occasionally missing valuable reliefs.

As an investor it is wise to be aware of the 3% surcharge that applies when purchasing second properties in your

The Property Tax Handbook for BRRR & BTL Investors

own name, and it will always apply for limited company purchasers.

The rates are different for commercial and residential property, as this book is focused toward residential property investment I have shown the current rates below.

Purchase price	Standard SDLT	With additional 3%
First £125,000 of the purchase price	0%	3%
Next £125,000	2%	5%
Next £675,000	5%	8%
Next £575,000	10%	13%
On amounts above £1.5m	12%	15%

In the later section on buying your first property we talk more on the topic of SDLT and run through some of the reliefs that are available.

The Property Tax Handbook for BRRR & BTL Investors

VAT

Fortunately for most residential property investors VAT should not be an issue due to the letting of residential property being exempt for VAT purposes. This means that you cannot register for VAT, charge VAT on your letting income, and also that you cannot reclaim any input VAT on expenses you incur.

Included within the category of residential property are house of multiple occupation (HMO) landlords. Therefore, even where your income from letting property exceeds the current £85,000 registration threshold for VAT you cannot actually register for VAT.

Exceptions to this are types of property trading activities such as deal sourcing, serviced accommodation and also commercial property letting on occasion. Where this income exceeds £85,000 in a 12 month period you will likely be required to register and start charging VAT.

Since as a property investor recovering VAT is usually not possible, we need to mention some of the potential areas where VAT can be saved. I have briefly included some of my favourite VAT tips for BRRR and BTL investors below.

Tax Tip: 5% VAT on HMO Conversions

Where you convert a single dwelling into a HMO rather than your builder having to charge 20% VAT on their labour and supplies, they might be able to charge just 5% VAT. On a £50,000 conversion with £10,000 of VAT, this could therefore save you £7,500.

Broadly the reduced 5% rate will apply where you are changing the number of dwellings, usually each room in a HMO will count as a separate dwelling. This means going from a single dwelling to a 5 bed HMO would count, as would converting a 2 bed HMO into a 6 bed. Converting a single house into 2 flats would also qualify.

There are only certain costs that qualify for the reduced rate, broadly those directly rating to the actual conversion itself.

Tax Tip: 5% VAT on Empty Properties

If you purchase a property that has been empty for two or more years the costs of refurbishing the property may be eligible for the 5% reduced rate of VAT.

Broadly speaking the property cannot have been occupied in the two years before it was purchased, and also no other renovation or alternation have taken place. Therefore, for properties that have been sitting empty for a long time this valuable VAT relief can help keep costs low!

The types of costs that benefit from the reduced 5% rate are:

- Work carried out to the fabric of the building and installing building materials
- Repairs and redecoration

- Improvement such as extensions and the installation of double glazing.

Costs incurred for installing white goods, carpets and fitted furniture would generally be chargeable to the 20% rate of VAT.

Inheritance Tax

If being subject to tax on all the money you make throughout your life wasn't bad enough on your eventual passing HMRC like to take one final stab at your wealth in the form of Inheritance Tax (IHT).

It's worth pointing out that IHT is a hugely complicated area and the best advice will always come from a specialist in the area, but I've covered some basics in the lightest of detail here so you know what you're up against.

IHT is payable on death, and on certain lifetime transfers such as to trusts. Here we will be focusing only on the death side of IHT.

Where a UK domiciled individual dies with net assets over £325,000 is it possible that IHT could be due at 40%. This £325,000 is termed as the nil rate band as works in a similar fashion to other tax-free allowances where amounts falling into this band are taxed at 0%.

The Property Tax Handbook for BRRR & BTL Investors

If you were to die with net assets of say £500,000, the first £325,000 would be covered the by nil rate band, with the remaining £175,000 charged to IHT at 40% giving a tax bill of £70,000.

For IHT purposes the estate value is based on net assets, as such any liabilities are deducted before calculating the amount subject to IHT. For a property investor this would include mortgages and other debt.

Example

Steve recently died leaving a portfolio of 10 BTL properties to his only child, he was not married. The total value of the properties was £1.5m, with £800,000 of mortgages secured against them.

When valuing Steve's estate, we deduct the value of the mortgages resulting in only £700,000 being taken into account for IHT purposes. As above he would qualify for the £325,000 nil rate band meaning that £375,000 would be the amount charged to IHT.

A similar method is also taken when valuing the shares in a property company for IHT purposes. Although a limited company may have £2m of property as assets, we would deduct the value of any liabilities to establish what the company was actually worth.

Where you leave all of your estate to your UK domiciled spouse there would usually not be any IHT to pay as these transfers are considered exempt. Where this transfer does take place the surviving spouse can utilise any of the unused nil rate band at the time of the first spouses death.

Example

Fred dies leaving an estate of £500,000 to his wife Linda. As they are all UK domiciled there is no IHT to pay on this transfer, however none of Fred's nil rate band has been used. As a result, when Linda subsequently dies 5 years later she (or rather, the people inheriting her property) will benefit from her £325,000 nil rate band, and also all of Fred's, resulting in £650,000 of net assets being taxed at 0%.

The Property Tax Handbook for BRRR & BTL Investors

Although not strictly relevant to property investors, it's worth mentioning the Residence Nil Rate Band to give you the best grasp on IHT.

If you leave a property which was your home to your direct lineal descendants (children, grandchildren, stepchildren, adopted and foster children, but not nieces, nephews or sibling) there will be an additional tax-free allowance available. It is currently £175,000 and applies in addition to the nil rate band where both are available.

Example

Owen has a BTL portfolio worth £400,000 and a main residence worth £175,000, all of which he leaves to his only child.

Here the £325,000 would be utilised against the BTL portfolio leaving £75,000 chargeable to IHT at 40% and also the residence nil rate band at £175,000 would be available to fully shield the value of the house from IHT.

The Property Tax Handbook for BRRR & BTL Investors

The residence nil rate band is gradually withdrawn where your overall estate value is more than £2m.

IHT is charged on assets held at death and also those gifts up to 7 years prior to death. It is a common tax myth that assets can all be gifted away in later life to avoid paying IHT. Rarely does this work as for property investors there would usually be CGT due as if the transaction took place at a market value rate, but for properties with no capital growth it might just be possible.

Tax Tip

There are a number of clever ways to save IHT usually involving trust structures. Examples of this include setting up an investment company with different classes of shares and putting the growth shares into trust, and also gifting an investment property into a trust, with the trust then subsequently distributing the property to the end beneficiary to take advantage of gift relief, providing exemption from paying any CGT on the transfer.

I could write another book on this topic entirely but if you do have assets over £500,000 including your main residence it is prudent to obtain IHT planning advice sooner rather than later.

The Property Tax Handbook for BRRR & BTL Investors

Important Reliefs and Exemptions

- Married couples: Assets left to a spouse are in the majority of cases free from IHT.

- Business property relief (BPR): Providing a business is deemed to be undertaking a trade then BPR should be available, providing relief from IHT at 50% or 100%. Other criteria apply therefore check with a professional adviser.

- Annual Allowance: £3000 of value per year can begiven without IHT becoming due.

- Potentially exempt transfer (PET): Providing you survive for 7 years following a gift then in the majority of cases no extra IHT will be due upon death. If you do not survive 7 years then it will be considered part of your estate on death resulting in additional taxes.

What type of property investor are you?

Most people that invest in property through BRR and BTL are just that, property investors. It's important to know the difference between what property trading is and what is investing.

The reason for distinguishing between the two is that property trading often has hugely beneficial tax reliefs available such as Business Asset Disposal Relief which allows for capital gains to be taxed at just 10%, Business Property Relief which can shield assets from 40% Inheritance tax, and also Gift Relief which can allow for assets to be gifted without any CGT.

There are also disadvantages when it comes to unincorporated property investors. Where you are considered to be property trading you will pay Income Tax and NIC on the profits on the sale of a property, this could be up to 62%!

The Property Tax Handbook for BRRR & BTL Investors

However, for a property investor selling a property the maximum rate would be only 28%. Property trading is where the property or land is bought with the intention of making a profit on the property itself, with the intention is to resell the property in a short to medium term timeframe.

Property investment is where a property is purchased with the intention of holding for long term rental income, the anticipation of future capital growth does not hinder the investment status. The key is around your intention when purchasing the property, did you plan to hold this for the long term, or were you planning to sell it on?

In determining whether a trader is indeed trading the 'Badges of Trade' are usually considered.

These are:
- Is there a profit motive? At the time of acquiring the property was there an intention of selling the property for a profit.

- How was the property acquired? If the property has been gifted or inherited, this is unlikely to be considered trading.

- How was the property financed? If there is short term finance in place such as a bridge this may hint towards trading. Note that if you subsequently refinance onto a mortgage this would hint towards investment.

- Frequency of transactions. If a large number of properties and been bought and sold this might indicate trading, however if properties are rarely sold this will support investment.

- How much time was there between purchase and sale? If there was only a short amount of time this would indicate trading, however selling a property after holding it for a number of years would support investment.
- Has the asset been changed? Where you have improved the asset by carrying out a

refurbishment prior to sale this can occasionally hint towards trading.

- What type of asset is it? Is the property typically a trading business such as a hotel, or is it already residential property?

Example

Lee purchases 5 new build flats in a single transaction from a developer. His intention at the time of purchase was to let the properties out as a long-term investment. Shortly after purchasing the properties, he is offered a deal that is too good to pass, he now sells one of the properties in order to realise funds for the new investment.

Although he purchased and subsequently sold the property in a short space of time, he does have a solid commercial rationale for doing so and as such should be considered a property investment business.

Example

The Property Tax Handbook for BRRR & BTL Investors

Mitchell purchased a property which was in a poor state and carried out a full refurbishment in order to get the property into a lettable condition. Following the strong uplift in the value of the property he decided to list the property for sale. The fact that he has changed the asset, likely purchased the property using short-term finance, and is now selling the property in a short space of time might indicate that he is a property trader, not an investment.

However, if there was a solid reason for selling the property, such as the intention to move away from the area, he was looking to re-invest elsewhere, or that he was disposing of his entire portfolio, this could indicate that he was running a property investment business.

Other potential circumstances that would be good reasons for a change of intention:
- You experience an unforeseen shortage in funds
- You receive an exceptionally good offer
- You move due to family, work or other reasons
- You separate from your partner

The Property Tax Handbook for BRRR & BTL Investors

- You inherit a property or other bereavement
- You wish to use the funds in another investment
- You have doubts over the property market n that location

There is no set criteria when it comes to establishing whether an individual is a property investment business or a property trader and as such it can be difficult in cases where there is a good argument for both. The best course of action would be to ensure all intentions are as well documented as possible, such as board minutes, memos with your accountant, business plans etc.

The difference between property trading and property investment is most relevant where you hold property in your own personal name, where a limited company is concerned the same flat rate of corporation tax applies regardless.

Other types of property activities that are taxed in a similar way to trading income include:

The Property Tax Handbook for BRRR & BTL Investors

- Operating properties as serviced accommodation, or furnished holiday lettings
- The development of property to sell on
- Deal sourcing, where you find deals and sell them on to investors for a fee

This means that if you carry out these activities in your own name you will pay Income tax on the profits in a year, and also NIC on the profits. The exception is serviced accommodation, which although you pay Income tax is generally only liable to Class 2 NIC.

The remainder of this book is focused on a property investment business as us property investors rarely sell our properties!

How to structure your property business?

Getting the right structure for your property business is crucial to maximise your wealth. There are a number of different mediums available to operate your property business through, in this chapter we will briefly cover the following:

- Running it through your own name (e.g. unincorporated)
- A traditional partnership
- A Limited liability partnership (LLP)
- A limited company
- A Smart Limited Company
- A group structure

Finding the right business structure will usually be a balance of tax and other commercial factors, such as what allows for the lowest cost of finance.

Unincorporated property business

As mentioned earlier on running a property business in your own name as an unincorporated landlord was popular up until 2017 when the tax system changed, and the section 24 mortgage interest restrictions came into play.

Up until this point a landlord could deduct all of their rental expenses and mortgage costs from the rent they had received and pay tax on this at 20%, 40% or 45% depending on which tax band the income fell within.

With the personal allowance and basic rate band totalling £50,000, this typically allowed for a landlord to receive circa £50,000 of rental profits and pay just £7,500 in tax, being left with £42,500 cash to enjoy.

For a husband/wife or partnership this was doubled, meaning a family unit could receive up to £100,000 and not get stung from a tax perspective.

Gradually introduced from April 2017 and now fully phased in from 6 April 2020 mortgage interest expenses are not an allowable cost when calculating the profits of a property rental business.

These changes have had a significant impact on landlords that:
- Have significant other income such as a salary
- Are higher rate taxpayers
- Receive child benefit
- Earn close to £100,000

The best way to illustrate the changes is through an example.

Example

Alex is a higher rate taxpayer with a small property portfolio generating him profits before finance costs of £30,000, the finance costs amount to £24,000, therefore the actual profit of the property business is £6,000.

The Property Tax Handbook for BRRR & BTL Investors

	Old system	New system
Profit before interest	30,000	30,000
Less: finance costs	(24,000)	0
Taxable profit	6,000	30,000
Tax @ 40%	2,400	12,000
Less: basic rate finance costs deduction	N/A	(4,800)
Tax payable	**2,400**	**7,200**

The changes have resulted in the total tax payable increasing from £2,400 up to £7,200!

The amount that attracts a basic rate tax deduction is the lowest of these three amounts:
- The total amount of finance costs incurred plus, any unrelieved finance costs brought forward
- The taxable profits of the property business

- Total taxable income for the year, not including dividend income, interest income, and other savings income; but after the personal allowance is deducted

Due to these restrictions buying property in your own name as an unincorporated landlord has become less popular as most investors are looking to acquire large portfolios.

If you were to run your property business as an unincorporated landlord you would need to file a self-assessment tax return each year.

The tax year in the UK runs from 6 April to the following 5 April, with a self-assessment tax return being due for income and gains within this period. The online filing deadline is 31 January following the end of the tax year and 31 October for paper filing.

The Property Tax Handbook for BRRR & BTL Investors

This means for the 2021/22 tax year, the tax year starts on 6 April 2021 and ends on 5 April 2022, with the self-assessment return being due on 31 January 2023.

I have summarised the pros and cons of buying through your own name here:

Pros

- Often lower finance costs and more mortgages available
- Lower Income tax rate for lower earnings (total income under £50,270)
- Lower accounting fees
- No information shown publicly on Companies House

Cons

- Finance costs are restricted for many landlords
- Lack of flexibility for tax planning, e.g. if you do not need the money no option to reinvest at a lower tax rate

The Property Tax Handbook for BRRR & BTL Investors

- No limited liability, if a tenant sues you are personally liable
- Does not allow for tax efficient IHT planning

Partnerships & LLP

Usually, property income that derives from joint held property amounts to an ordinary property business. The total rental income and expenditure here is just split by the ownership of the property, and then these amounts are included on the property section of the individual tax return, inclusive of any other rental income you may receive personally.

For a partnership to exist the activities must amount to more than just the joint letting of property. The Partnership Act of 1890 defines a partnership as 'The relationship which subsists between persons carrying on a business in common with a view of profit'. What this means is that there ought to be more than the passive collection of rents in order for there to be a bona fide partnership.

Activities which will help with evidencing a partnership would include:

- Separate partnership bank account
- Partnership agreement in place

The Property Tax Handbook for BRRR & BTL Investors

- Dealing with tenants
- Managing repairs
- Chasing any unpaid rents
- Finding new properties

A partnership is taxed in a similar way to an individual in that Income tax is due on the rental profits. Mortgage interest costs are also restricted in the same way as an individual. The biggest benefit in there being a partnership for Income tax purposes is that partnership profits can be split as the partners see fit, this contrasts the tax position of jointly owned property.

Property which is jointly owned is split directly in accordance with the legal (or beneficial) ownership proportion. Therefore, if there is £10,000 of rental income between two 50/50 joint owners each of them would be assessed on their 50% share. The issue here is that for couples it is quite common for one to be a higher rate taxpayer, with the other a lower rate taxpayer. What happens in cases like this is that the higher rate taxpayer pays tax at 40% on their share (likely even more when the finance cost restriction is considered) and the lower rate taxpayer pays tax at 20%.

Owning property jointly can clearly have expensive tax ramifications, hence the appeal of a property partnership. Where there is a partnership as mentioned above, the income and gains of the partnership can be split each year as the discretion of the partners.

This would mean that in the case above where you have a higher rate taxpayer and a lower rate taxpayer both in the partnership, it would make sense to allocate more the rental profits to the basic rate taxpayer who pays tax at 20%, than the 40% taxpayer. A property partnership allows for just this to happen.

The members of a partnership will need to complete the partnership sections of their self-assessment tax returns, and the partnership itself will need some complete its own return with its own UTR, this is called a SA800.

The Property Tax Handbook for BRRR & BTL Investors

A Limited liability partnership (LLP) is very similar to an ordinary partnership with the exception that they benefit from limited liability, this means that the personal assets of the partners are not directly as risk should anything happen in the property business. Other benefits of an LLP include the ability to the LLP to directly own property, in an ordinary partnership the actual ownership of the property will be a mixture of the members.

It is worth noting that an LLP will need to file annual accounts and a confirmation statement to Companies House, these result in an additional administration and accounting fees than would be the case with an ordinary partnership.

When it comes to holding residential property both an ordinary partnership and an LLP have equal merits but owing to the finance cost restrictions impact both alike, they are not suitable for the majority of property investors looking to grow significant portfolios.

Limited Companies

Following the tax changes that have impacted other property investment vehicles, limited companies remain attractive due to the ability for 100% of the mortgage interest and other finance costs being deductible for tax purposes.

Currently the Corporation Tax rate of 19% is lower than rates that would be applicable to investors who invest via their own name or a partnership, this allows for rental profits to be accumulated in the most tax efficient manner.

In a similar way to an LLP a limited company is its own distinct and separate legal entity which can enter into contracts in its own right. This means that from a legal and tax point of view the owners of the business and the company are completely separate, this would mean that in the event of the business failing or a tenant attempting to sue a landlord, it would only be the assets of the company at risk, and not the personal assets of the business owner.

The Property Tax Handbook for BRRR & BTL Investors

The main exception to this is where a personal guarantee is given by the directors of the business. This is where the directors are personally guaranteeing the liability of the company, and as such should the company not satisfy the obligations of the company, can be held personally liable. In property investment it is very common for the directors of a limited company to be required to give a personal guarantee on a mortgage taken out via a limited company.

A limited company has other advantages in that they are extremely flexible when it comes to ownership structure, with the ability to add and remove joint venture partners without issue.

Each year a limited company will need to file annual accounts with Companies House, along with a confirmation statement, a Corporation tax return also needs to be submitted to HMRC. The remainder of this book is written in the context of a limited company as this is now the most common ownership structure.

The Property Tax Handbook for BRRR & BTL Investors

Setting up your limited company

Before you can start to buy property will you need a new limited company set up specifically to hold property in.

The reason for this is that you would likely not want to hold property within a trading company as it will hinder the availability of tax reliefs such as Business asset disposal relief and business property relief which can save you CGT and IHT later down the line.

Other factors to consider are that all trading business carry a degree of risk and now more than ever the threat of legal action from a disgruntled customer is real, therefore holding all of your valuable investment properties in the same entity that carries on this activity could easily prove an expensive mistake.

The Property Tax Handbook for BRRR & BTL Investors

Lastly, when it comes to obtaining mortgages for buy to let properties the vast majority of lenders will prefer to lend to a property company that only holds investment properties. If there is a sign of other trading history, you may find it slightly more challenging to get the finance you need.

For the reasons above we set up new limited companies, often termed as SPVs (special purpose vehicles) to buy and hold property in.

A standard SPV is relatively straightforward to set up and can be incorporated within one to two working days. However, a company can be set up in a variety of different ways and care must be taken to ensure you get the right structure in place.

When setting up a limited company you will be asked to select a Standard Industrial Classification (SIC) code. These are fundamentally used by the Office of National Statistics (ONS) to track the activity of what companies are doing. However, they do also have other uses in

The Property Tax Handbook for BRRR & BTL Investors

demonstrating to mortgage lenders and HMRC the activities of a company in particular.

If you are purchasing a property using a mortgage, the lender will quite often be very anal about what SIC code is shown on Companies House, therefore it pays to get this right.

Previously before we have had to set up a completely separate limited company for a client due to the lender seeing that historically the SIC code was that of a trading business and not investment. It is important that this SIC code is used at the time of incorporation, otherwise you may find yourself needing to set up a new limited company.

The main SIC codes for buy to let and BRRR are as follows:
- 68100 - Buying and selling of own real estate
- 68209 - Other letting and operating of own or leased real estate

- 68320 - Management of real estate on a fee or contract basis

I have a webinar recording on how to set up a limited company, if you want a copy email proof that you have left an Amazon review to sacha@jsmpartners.co.uk

Simple Limited Company

A simple limited company is incorporated at Companies House with a single class of ordinary shares. Most companies only have one kind of shares, called ordinary shares. Ordinary shares represent the company's basic voting rights and reflect the equity ownership of a company. Ordinary shares typically carry one vote per share and each share gives equal right to dividends. These shares also give right to the distribution of the company's assets in the event of winding-up or sale.

Setting up a simple limited can be fine for some investors with very basic requirements, such as those who are not married, have no children, and are in business on their own. Investors that fall outside of this may be better placed setting up a Smart limited company.

Example

ABC Property Company Ltd was set up with two husband and wife shareholders, John and Claire. John is an IT contractor and earns £90,000 per annum, Claire is a part-time teacher earning £20,000 per annum. They have 5 properties in the company producing decent rental profits.

A few years down the line after allowing the rental profits to accumulate they wish to extract £30,000 to pay for a lavish holiday. As they both own the company in 50% equal proportions, they will both be taxed on 50% of the dividend each, being £15,000. This will have a significant impact from a tax perspective.

As John is a higher rate taxpayer, he will pay tax at an effective rate of 60% on some of the dividend income, this is because as his dividends exceed the £100,000 mark, he begins to lose his personal allowance. On the remainder of the dividends above his £2,000 dividend allowance, he will pay tax at 32.5%. We don't need detailed calculations here to show that he's paying a lot in tax! Prior to taking the dividend he would be paying circa £23,500 in Income tax, after taking the £15,000 dividend this will shoot up to £28,725. This is an increase of £5,225.

If we contrast this with Claire who is a basic-rate rate taxpayer, she will receive the first £2,000 tax-free by using her dividend allowance. The remaining £13,000 will be taxed at 7.5% giving rise to an addition Income tax liability of just £975.

Clearly here the better option would have been to give Claire all of the dividend income to utilise her remaining basic rate band. This was previously possibly by utilising dividend waivers where John would essentially waive his dividend of £15,000, so that there would then be enough retained profits for Claire to receive a £30,000 dividend. These have been subject to a number of challenges by

HMRC in recent years and should be avoided where possible.

However, there is a solution to this problem, a smart limited company as described below.

Smarter Limited Company

Following on from the example with John and Claire previously, however instead of setting up a standard limited company they sought expert guidance and set up a smarter limited company.

Rather than having just the single class of ordinary shares, they now have two share classes, called A class shares, and B class shares. The articles of association are distinctly drafted so that the company is allowed to vote different levels of dividends to different shareholders.

John owns the A shares with Claire owning the B shares. Aside from the name and ability to receive different dividends the shares are identical to before in that they both own and control 50% of the company each.

The Property Tax Handbook for BRRR & BTL Investors

Now when it comes to the extraction of the same £30,000 the tax position will be significantly different.

John will receive £2,000 to utilise his dividend allowance. The remaining £28,000 will be received by Claire on her B class shares. The tax will be as follows, £2,000 tax-free with the dividend allowance and the remaining £26,000 will be taxed at 7.5% giving total income tax of £1,950.

Compared with the above where the total tax paid was an eye-watering £6,200, this is a saving of £4,250! This wouldn't be a one-time saving, this would be in point each time dividends are taken from the company.

This is one of the main benefits of the smarter company structure, in that dividends can be paid in different proportions to different shareholders. Where you or your spouse pay tax at different rates the benefits can be huge. The same is true where you have business partners with one member perhaps not wanting to draw any dividends, or different levels of input in the business.

Other benefits are available especially when it comes to Inheritance tax planning. As we mentioned earlier the net asset value of the company is generally what counts for the purposes of IHT, therefore as the values of the properties continue to rise over time as does the value of them company.

A solution here is to create special classes of shares such that some of the shares do not have the rights to any future capital growth in the company, and others do. This can be done at any time during the company's life however for the best and most effective tax outcome it is best out into place at the time of the company's inception.

The main outcome is to move as much value from your estate into the estate of the younger generation, whilst still retaining rights to income from the shares (by way of dividends) and perhaps control of the company such that the younger generation do not squander the family wealth through poor investment decisions.

Example

Daniel is the owner of D Property Investments Ltd, a company which owns 20 buy to lets in the North East of England. The current value of the company is £4m in total assets, less £2.5m of loans, suggesting that the net asset value of the company is in the region of £1.5m.

Daniel receives newly issued B class shares, and the original shares are re-designated as A Shares. Following this the Articles of Association of the company are amended so that the holder of the B shares are only entitled to dividends and capital on the winding up of the company, and only to the extent that A shares have already received £1.5m. The B shares can then be given by Daniel into a discretionary trust for the benefit of his children or grandchildren.

In say 20 years time when the Daniel has passed and the company has increased in value to £2.5m in net assets a lot of the value of the company will fall outside of his estate and into the trust. If Daniel had taken £1m of dividends from the company, this would be taken from the value of the value of his shares, meaning only £500,000 is taxable at up to 40%, not the £2.5m which would otherwise have been.

This was an example of an already established company that was able to benefit from this type of restructuring to save a significant amount of tax, establishing this type of structure from the incorporation does give the best results.

Example

Steve and Steph are looking to build a large portfolio for their children however they already have other substantial assets and as such are looking to reduce their IHT exposure.

After receiving advice from a specialist, they set up a smarter limited company with the following share classes with the following rights:

- A shares; rights to income, rights to vote, and rights to receive initial capital with no further rights to capital

- B shares; rights to capital on once the capital value of A shares repaid and rights to future capital growth

This arrangement allows for Steve and Steph to control the company whilst building up the property portfolio and also take dividend income to fund their retirement. The actual capital growth of the company belongs to the owners of the B shares, which could either be given directly to the younger generation or placed into trust for the ultimate protection of assets.

This type of tax planning is very complicated and should not be undertaken on a DIY basis, we've made it sound simple above by omitting a lot of the complicated details, however for this to be effective you will need professional guidance.

Group Structures

The final type of ownership structure we will cover is group companies. The individual set up of each company will be as above in that they will either have a single class of shares or numerous classes with different rights.

The specifics would be heavily dependent on what the companies are doing, and the values involved. Typically, when companies are set up the shareholders are the people running the business. You can see a standard company structure below.

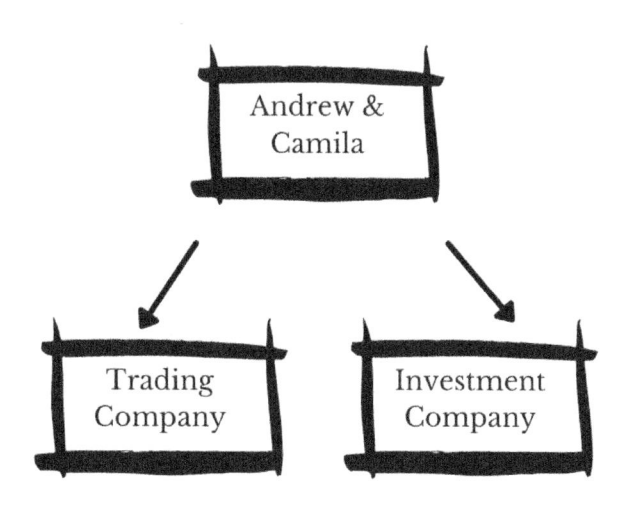

```
            ┌─────────────┐
            │  Andrew &   │
            │   Camila    │
            └─────────────┘
              ↙         ↘
   ┌──────────┐       ┌──────────┐
   │ Trading  │       │Investment│
   │ Company  │       │ Company  │
   └──────────┘       └──────────┘
```

The Property Tax Handbook for BRRR & BTL Investors

For example, 10 years ago Andrew and Camila set up a cake making business as a limited company, when the company was set up they created a single class of ordinary shares and issued 10 shares, having 5 each.

Over the years the business has become very profitable, building modest cash reserves of £200,000. They both wish to utilise these cash reserves to invest in property and have heard that the easiest way to get the cash out would be to borrow it from the company personally, or to take it out as a dividend.

If they were to take the money out as a dividend personally, they would pay tax at rates of up to 38.1% depending on their other income for the tax year. This would be a very inefficient way of taking the funds out.

A slightly better way could be to borrow the money from their limited company as a directors' loan, however where this loan is still outstanding 9 months and 1 day from the end of the company's accounting year end, there would be a 32.5% temporary tax charge (known as S.455 tax).

This would be payable at this time and would only be refunded to the company when the loan has been repaid, even then it's 9 months and 1 day from the end of the accounting period in which the loan was repaid, meaning that there will be a long period of time with this significant amount of money held up in the government coffers.

Another point to note is that where the loan from the company to the director exceeds £10,000, the company will need to charge interest on the loan at a rate of at least 2.25% (HMRC's official rate of interest), failure to do so would result in the loan being considered a beneficial loan with the need to file a P11D, the individual receiving the loan having an Income tax charge, and also the company have a Class 1A NIC liability. I'm sure you can agree it's probably best to avoid this happening and find a better solution.

An acceptable solution

A solution which is the short term would achieve an acceptable outcome from a tax perspective would be for the baking business to loan the £200,000 to the newly formed SPV.

The loan should be documented with a loan agreement in place, there is no requirement for an interest rate to be charged, and it would usually not be worth doing so as you would save Corporation tax at 19% in one company only to pay 19% Corporation tax on the interest income in the other company.

If one of the companies has losses brought forward or is overseas resident that does change things and would present a planning opportunity.

The reason this is acceptable for the short term only is that at some point this loan does need to be repaid. Over time with each year the company's excess profits being added to this loan so that more properties can be purchased the value will keep going up and could easily become a £1m problem over a decade or two.

If the baking company were to run into financial difficulty or be sued then the £1m loan to the property company is an asset of the trading company and could potentially be called in, this may force the property company to have to sell some properties or refinance in a rushed bit to repay some of the loan.

Alternatively, if Andrew and Camila wanted to sell the baking business to live a life of financial freedom via property, they would have the problem of their being a £1m loan sitting on the balance sheet of the baking business. This loan balance would make it very difficult to sell the business, if not impossible.

The loan could be written off however this would have the effect of giving the baking business a £1m capital loss which it would likely not have sufficient profits to set the loss against, giving it capital losses to carry forward. In the property business the £1m capital gain would arise, giving a tax charge at 19%. Even just writing the loans off could cost as much as £190,000 in tax alone.

Loaning money between companies is generally fine on a short-term basis but is not a sound long term strategy from a tax perspective.

A Better Solution

The problem with the above was that the two companies (the trading company and the investment company) were owned by individual persons, being Andrew and Camila. If instead of them both owning the shares directly in each company, they set up a new holding company to make a group of companies for tax purposes the results would be far different.

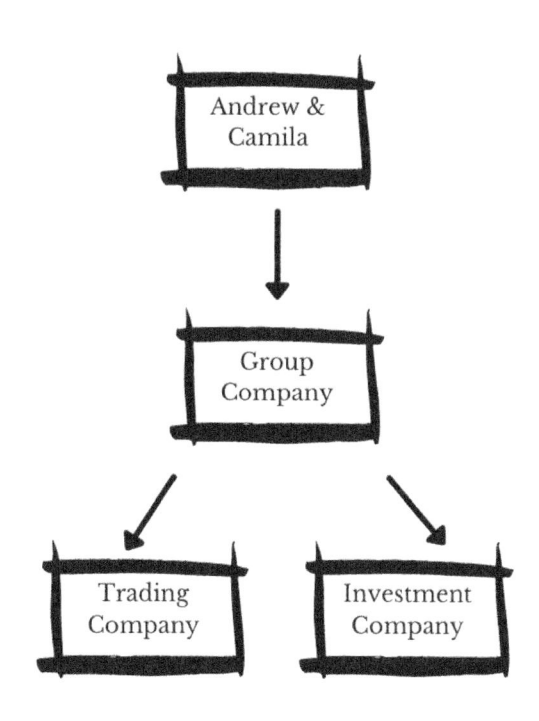

```
          ┌─────────────┐
          │  Andrew &   │
          │   Camila    │
          └──────┬──────┘
                 │
                 ▼
          ┌─────────────┐
          │    Group    │
          │   Company   │
          └──┬───────┬──┘
            ╱         ╲
           ▼           ▼
  ┌─────────────┐  ┌─────────────┐
  │   Trading   │  │ Investment  │
  │   Company   │  │   Company   │
  └─────────────┘  └─────────────┘
```

Following on from the example above with Andrew and Camila. Instead of setting up a simple company as they did, they spoke to a tax professional and told them of their plans to run the trading business and re-invest the profits into property via a separate company. Based on their circumstances and the forecasts presented the tax advisor suggested they set up a different type of structure, a group structure.

The benefits of having a group structure in place are as follows:

- A group of companies can be in the same group for SDLT purposes, this allows for assets usually charged to SDLT can be moved between companies free of SDLT. For this to be available companies must broadly be owned by the same corporate body, with that corporate body holding at least 75% of the share capital.

- Losses in one company can be offset against profits in another company. Group relief allows losses to be surrendered from loss-making companies to profitable companies in the same 75% group. For instance, if the trading business were to have a bad year and make a loss, these losses could be offset against profits in the property company.

- Companies can elect to be treated as a single entity for VAT purposes, by forming a VAT group. A VAT group is treated in the same way as a single taxable person registered for VAT on its own. The registration is made in the name of the 'representative member'. The representative member is responsible for completing and submitting a single VAT Return and making VAT payments or receiving VAT refunds on behalf of the group. However, all the members of the group remain jointly and severally liable for any VAT debts. The advantages to forming a VAT group are that supplies can move between companies without the need to account for VAT and that the administration burden is reduced.

- The substantial shareholding exemption applies to companies and exempts certain gains from Corporation tax on the disposal of shares. Broadly the company being sold must have been a trading company, which is usually held to be a company that does not have more than 20% non-trading activities. Providing all of the criteria are met then the shareholding can be sold free of tax with the group company making the disposal, receiving 100% of the sales proceeds.

- Funds can be moved between the group tax efficiently. Where there is a group structure in place dividends can usually be paid up to the group company without any tax due on the dividend income. This allows for profits and cash to be moved out from the riskier trading business, into other entities where the money can be ring-fenced and invested into assets.

The Property Tax Handbook for BRRR & BTL Investors

What taxes apply when buying property?

When buying a property, the main tax in point is going to be Stamp Duty Land Tax (SDLT) and therefore I thought it would be wise to dedicate a short section to this tax in its entirety. There are many crossovers between SDLT, LTT (Wales), and LBTT (Scotland) however the focus here is on how SDLT works in England.

Depending on when you read this book the temporary SDLT holiday may still be in place, as it is applicable up until the end of June. However, in order to ensure this book is concise and relevant the details on the temporary SDLT holiday have been omitted.

The Property Tax Handbook for BRRR & BTL Investors

Purchase price	Property investor rate
Up to £125,000	3%
Next £125,000	5%
Next £675,000	8%
Next £575,000	13%
On amounts above £1.5m	15%

If the entity purchasing the property is Non-UK Resident there will usually be a 2% surcharge on top of the rates above, this has been applicable on all transactions since 1 April 2021.

Example

Joshua buys a residential property via his limited company for £125,000. The SDLT here is a flat 3% resulting in £3,750 of tax due 14 days from the effective completion date of the transaction.

The effective date will usually be the date the transaction is completed but can be earlier if a contract or agreement for sale or lease has been 'substantially performed' at an earlier stage. This can happen, for example, where a tenant or purchaser is allowed into occupation, perhaps to carry out fit out works, before the sale or lease is completed.

Example

ABC Limited purchases a large 4 bed property for £250,000. The SDLT here would be the first £125,000 @ 3% giving £3,750, and then the second £125,000 @ 5% giving £6,250. The total SDLT due here would therefore be £10,000.

Multiple Dwellings Relief

You can claim relief when you buy more than one dwelling where a transaction or a number of linked transactions include freehold or leasehold interests in more than one dwelling.

If you claim relief, to work out the rate of tax HMRC charge:

- Divide the total amount paid for the properties by the number of dwellings
- Work out the tax due on this figure

- Multiply this amount of tax by the number of dwellings

The minimum rate of tax under the relief is 1% of the amount paid for the dwellings.

When two or more property transactions involve the same buyer and seller, they count as 'linked' for SDLT. HMRC may count people connected to a buyer or seller as being the same buyer or seller.

If 2 or more transactions are treated as linked, then the buyer pays any SDLT due on the total value of all linked transactions. This may mean that they pay a higher rate of SDLT than if the transactions are counted individually.

Example

Property Investment Company Ltd purchase 3 houses for £500,000 at the same time from the same seller, for SDLT purposes this is treated as a linked transaction meaning that SDLT is charged on the full £500,000.

The SDLT here would therefore be £30,000. Calculated as:

- First £125,000 @ 3%
- Between £125,000 and £250,000 @ 5%
- Above £250,000 @ 8%

This is a lot more than would be payable under the normal rules if each property were purchased separately, to provide relief towards this MDR is usually available.

Three houses for £500,000 gives an average house price of £166,666. The SDLT is calculated on a single property using the average value, here this gives SDLT of £5,833. The £5,833 is then multiplied by 3 to give SDLT of £17,499. Here claiming Multiple Dwelling Relief saves SDLT of £12,501!

The minimum amount under MDR is 1% of the £500,000, being £5,000, as the amount calculated above is more than this the higher amount is used.

For the purposes of MDR a "dwelling" means a building or part of a building which is suitable for use as a single dwelling or is in the process of being constructed or adapted for such use. Therefore, the scope of MDR is wide reaching in that it can apply where there are substantial outbuildings, or where there are several self-contained units.

Example

Property Investments Ltd is purchasing a block of 10 flats for £900,000 from a single developer.

As above, this would be considered a 'linked transaction' meaning SDLT is calculated using the aggregate value of the flats. Using the £900,000 to calculate the SDLT would give a SDLT liability of £62,000.

Using MDR to calculate the gain would substantially bring down the amount of SDLT to just £27,000. It certainly pays to know when MDR might be available as clearly the savings can be significant.

The Property Tax Handbook for BRRR & BTL Investors

Commercial Rates

There's another relief available for purchases involving multiple units, here it's the ability to claim that commercial property SDLT rates apply to the transaction rather than residential. For this relief to be available 6 or more residential properties must be bought together in a single transaction.

Commercial rates of SDLT also apply where you are buying mixed-use properties, such as a flat above with a shop below.

Purchase price	Commercial SDLT Rate
Up to £150,000	0%
Between £150,001 and £250,000	2%
Above £250,000	5%

Example

Property Investment Ltd purchase a block of 15 flats from the same vendor for £1.7m.

We will need to calculate the SDLT using the normal method first, as it is a linked transaction SDLT will be calculate on the £1.7m as a single sum. The SDLT due on this basis would be £168,750.

Calculating the same liability however this time claiming MDR. The SDLT due under this calculation is £51,000.

Because there are 6 or more properties being bought in a single or series of linked transactions we can also calculate the SDLT liability applying the commercial rates of SDLT. The full £1,700,000 is charged to SDLT in line with the marginal rates above, this gives a liability of £74,500.

We can claim the calculation that gives the lowest SDLT liability and therefore in this case we will opt for MDR to apply. It's important that your professional advisors are undertaking these calculations as the difference between what the SDLT would have been (£168,750) and the amount due whilst claiming MDR (£51,000) is a significant sum, £117,750!

The Property Tax Handbook for BRRR & BTL Investors

Probate Relief

Another relief which is not very well known is SDLT relief available where a property trader purchases a property from the personal representatives of a deceased individual.

The conditions that must be met are as follows:

- The purchase is in the course of a business that consists of purchasing dwellings from the personal representatives of deceased individuals

- The deceased individual occupied the dwelling as his main or only residence at some time in the two years ending with the date of their death and

- The area of land acquired does not exceed the permitted area – Permitted area being 10,000sqm

This relief is great for those that are doing flips as the business of the company acquiring the property must be that of a property trader, meaning the properties cannot be held for investment, they must be sold on.

However, where you have two property companies, one that holds properties as long term investments, and one that is a property flipping company, there is nothing to suggest that the property cannot be purchased in the trading company where the refurb takes place and then sell it to the investment company where it is let long term.

The SDLT saving will be withdrawn if you do any of the following:
- Spend more than the permitted amount on the refurbishment of the dwelling or
- Grants a lease or licence of the dwelling or
- Permits any of your principals or employees, or any person connected with any of its principals or employees, to occupy the dwelling

The permitted amount in relation to the refurbishment of a dwelling is £10,000 or 5% of the consideration for the acquisition, whichever is the greater, up to a maximum of £20,000.

The refurbishment of a dwelling means carrying out works that enhance or are intended to enhance its value but does not include cleaning or work to ensure it meets minimum safety standards.

This therefore means that all of the costs of ripping out the property and bringing the property back up to a safe standard are not included within the 'permitted amount' above. It is definitely worth exploring whether this relief is available on a purchase as the savings can be significant. If you were to purchase a £200,000 property which qualified for Probate relief the SDLT saving would be £7,500!

Uninhabitable Properties

Where a property is deemed to be uninhabitable at the time of purchase the 3% SDLT surcharge will not be applicable, and in some cases the property will not be deemed as residential property at all, and instead charged to SDLT under the non-residential rates.

The most contentious issue here is what constitutes an uninhabitable property and what doesn't, there is no set criteria and each case is considered on its merits, however below is some guidance from HMRC and the relevant tribunal decisions.

For example, a residential property that is no longer habitable as a dwelling as a result of dereliction would not be residential property on the basis that it is not suitable for use as a dwelling.

However, there is a clear distinction between derelict property and a dwelling that is essentially habitable, but in need of modernisation, renovation or repair, which can be addressed without materially changing the structural nature of the property.

In this case, if the building was used as a dwelling at some point previously and permission to use as a dwelling continues to exist at the effective date of transaction, it will be considered suitable for use as a dwelling. Whether a property is derelict to the extent that it no longer comprises a dwelling is a question of fact and should only apply to a small minority of buildings.

The removal of, for example, a bathroom or kitchen facilities before sale will not be regarded as making a building unsuitable for use as a dwelling. These are internal fittings and would not constitute structural changes to the dwelling that would mean the building is no longer suitable for use as a dwelling.

A new kitchen or bathroom suite could be fitted relatively quickly and cheaply and is a common improvement to a dwelling. Likewise, substantial repairs required to windows or a roof would also not make the building unsuitable for use as a dwelling. Other examples of issues which may be easily addressed in the short term include the need to switch services back on and dealing with an infestation of pests.

During the First Tier Tribunal case of Bewley it was stated that "a dwelling will, as a minimum, contain facilities for personal hygiene, the consumption of food and drink, the storage of personal belongings, and a place for an individual to rest and to sleep".

Some headline factors to consider are:
- Has the property been vacant for a number of years?
- Is there gas or electricity in the property?
- Are there floorboards down upstairs?
- Are there signs of asbestos or other similar materials?
- Is the property due to be demolished?
- Are there significant structural issues?

If these factors are present in a property you are purchasing definitely speak to your accountant or solicitor about the possibility of paying a reduced amount of SDLT.

For those that have purchased a property that you feel was uninhabitable at the time of purchase the SDLT return can be amended up to 12 months from the date of the transaction. There is also the scope to claim back up to 4 years by claiming **SDLT Overpayment Relief**.

With SDLT it really can be a specialist area and it pays to ensure you are taking sound tax advice from a specialist in the area. Now you know the basics of some of the most valuable SDLT reliefs you are well equipped to hold your professional advisors to task in ensuring the most beneficial reliefs are claimed.

Running a limited company

Now that you've got a limited company set up, what do you need to do with it?! Well aside from buying property there are a number of things you ought to be aware of in order to maximise your chances of successfully running your limited company. As property investors it's easy to focus on finding properties but staying on top of your numbers, filing your taxes ahead of schedule, and being generally organised really are important when building a property business.

How are limited company profits calculated?

The profits of a limited company are calculated in line with Generally Accepted Accounting Principles (GAAP). We won't go into detail on them here but the main concept to take away is that profits and losses are calculated using the accruals basis, defined over the next few pages.

Revenue Expenditure

Revenue expenditure is that which relates to the day to day running of your business, such as letting agent fees or gardening costs. For such expenditure to be an allowable deduction, it must be incurred 'wholly and exclusively' for the purposes of your property business, meaning that it must be for the benefit of the business and not benefit you personally.

The effect of an expense being allowable is that it reduces your taxable profits upon which tax is calculated. An expense that is disallowed is not deducted from taxable profits meaning you pay 100% of the cost.

If there is an expense that benefits you personally in addition to the business this is termed as being 'mixed use' expenditure. All 'mixed use' expenditure should be split between the business and personal element on a just and reasonable basis. An example of 'mixed use' expenditure would be having a painter repaint your own home as well as a rental property.

The Property Tax Handbook for BRRR & BTL Investors

The amount that relates to the rental property should be identified, with only this amount being claimable as a deduction from profits.

If the identifiable business element cannot be identified then it is said to be 'dual purpose' and none of the expense can be deducted. Ordinary clothing costs are a typical example of dual purpose expenditure because you require them to remain warm and decent. Note, this is different to safety clothing and equipment which would be an allowable deduction.

It is these revenue costs that are set against rental income received to arrive at your taxable profit for the year. Therefore, the more allowable expenditure you have the lower your taxable profit and associated tax bill will be. Where there is VAT on a cost which cannot be recovered the whole amount inclusive of VAT can be deducted. This will usually be the case for a landlord due to the letting of residential property being exempt from VAT.

Accruals Basis

Profits are usually calculated under the 'accruals basis'; this means that income and expenses are recorded when they are incurred.

For example, if a landlord had new carpets fitted in March 2020 the cost would be recorded when the carpets are fitted, even if the invoice is not yet received or paid. Rental payments that have been received in advance would not be accounted for until the month it relates to.

Example

A new tenant takes out a tenancy on 1 January 2020 and pays 6 months rent upfront. The rental income to be recognised would be as follows.

The monthly rent for January, February, and March would be included in the tax year 2019/20 and included on the tax return for this year.

The remaining months prepaid; April, May, and June would **not be included** in the 2020/21 tax year, despite the cash being received. These funds would be recorded as rental income on the tax return for the next tax year being 2020/21.

In accounting lingo this is 'deferred income', meaning money received for goods or services not yet provided or delivered. The rental property has not been provided for the whole 6 months yet and, as such, the income must be split between 'earned income' and 'deferred income'.

Capital Expenditure

Capital expenditure is that which relates to the acquisition or enhancement of an asset with an expected life of over 2 years. An asset with an expected life of under a year would be a revenue expense. If the life is between one and two years it requires some judgement to determine the best way to record the expense.

An extension built on a rental property would be a capital expense on the basis that the property is being enhanced and should last a lot longer than 2 years. A new laptop would also be a capital expense on the basis that it relates to the acquisition of an asset expected to last over 2 years.

As a rule of thumb capital expenses will not be deductible from profits, either in the accounts or for tax purposes.

Depreciation and capital allowances would usually be available to account for these capital expenses. Depreciation is an accountant's way of giving a deduction for the cost of an asset within the accounts.

The purpose of depreciation is to match the fall in value of a capital asset with the benefit it brings to the business. This is because although the expense has been incurred now, the actual benefits of the owning the asset will be enjoyed over a period of time, often several years. This is the main principle behind the accruals method of accounting which is outlined later in this section.

Example

Keith bought a car which is to be used within his business and expects it to last 4 years. Rather than recognise the full amount in the year of purchase he will depreciate the car over the 4 years he expects it to be used within the business.

Each year 25% of the cars cost would be recorded in the accounts as depreciation effectively matching the cost with the benefit it brings to the business. There are many different methods available for calculating depreciation with this being a simple example.

It makes sense if you think of it as a matching exercise. Keith will be driving the car around visiting rental properties which are bringing in revenue and profits, so part of the cost of the car should be recorded against this.

Depreciation is only given where assets used within the business or trade, and are likely going to fall in value as a result of this business use.

The Property Tax Handbook for BRRR & BTL Investors

Properties purchased for investment purposes are never usually depreciated for a couple of reasons, the most prominent being the fact that on average house prices increase over time regardless of any business use.

Property Investment

The purchase of residential property by a landlord will be capital expenditure, as would any associated costs incurred that relate to purchasing the property.

Typically associated costs would include:
- Legal fees
- Stamp duty land tax
- Estate agent's fees
- Surveying fees
- Valuation costs

Example

Keith purchased a house for £100,000, also incurring Stamp Duty Land Tax of £3,000 and legals of £1,000. All of this is capital expenditure and will only be deductible when he comes to sell the property at a point in future.

A UK resident individual selling a property (a capital asset) would be liable to CGT on any increase in value (a capital gain).

Improvement (enhancement) expenditure is also considered as a capital expense and can be added to the original cost of the asset.

Providing the improvement expenditure is still reflected in condition of the property on sale this can be included as part of the asset cost for capital gains tax purposes. Following the example above, if the property was in a state of disrepair and could not be let in it's current state and £20,000 was spent on bringing it to a marketable condition then this would likely be considered capital expenditure.

If 10 years later the property is sold the cost would be £100,000 + £3,000 + £1,000 + £20,000 = £124,000.

This amount would be the allowable base cost for CGT purposes assuming no further capital expenditure had taken place.

Receiving a tax deduction for capital expenditure on residential property will only happen when you dispose of the property - this means that if you never dispose of the asset you will never receive a tax deduction for the capital expenditure. Even if you do sell in 20 years' time inflation will have eroded the real value of any costs incurred. For this reason, it's usually best to try and claim costs as a revenue expense against rental income where there is scope to do so.

It's important to keep good quality records of all capital expenditure and store them somewhere safe. Very often invoices get lost which can make it a lot harder to claim any capital expenses when the property is sold!

Abortive Expenditure

Where you incur expenditure in relation the purchase of a property (which would be deemed as capital expenditure) and the purchase does not go ahead, this is known as abortive expenditure.

With capital expenditure you only receive tax relief on the costs at the point at which you dispose of the capital asset, however where you did not purchase the asset there would of course be no asset to sell and thus obtain tax relief. Therefore when you incur abortive expenditure you do not obtain tax relief on it.

Capital Allowances

Now you know all about depreciation and how it works in accounting, forget it. In the world of tax depreciation is not an allowable deduction from profits. Depreciation is often the first expense that is 'added back', meaning the expense is added to profit, resulting in a higher profit figure for tax purposes! Before you take to the streets in protest of how unfair this may seem, there is a form of 'tax allowable depreciation' available, known as capital allowances.

Capital allowances are usually available to provide tax relief on the purchase of qualifying plant, machinery, fixtures and fittings, and integral features. Determining what does and does not qualifying is literally a book in its own right, see 'Capital Allowances: Transactions and Planning: 2020/21' by Martin Wilson and Steve Bone for a 624 page comprehensive guide.

The Property Tax Handbook for BRRR & BTL Investors

Most relevant to residential property landlords will be the capital allowances available on assets that are used within a property business, known as 'plant and machinery'.

Expenditure on 'plant and machinery' which is going to be used within a residential dwelling property will rarely qualifying for capital allowances. This means the cost of installing carpets or supplying a fridge will not be eligible for any form of tax deduction resulting in a higher effective cost. For certain items the replacement of domestic items relief will apply, however this does not provide any relief for the initial cost of the capital asset.

Do note that capital allowances will never be available for a residential property landlord towards the cost of the property itself, only 'plant and machinery' used within the business. Expenditure on assets such as laptops, iPads, and mobile phones will usually qualify for capital allowances, meaning a deduction will be available to lower profits subject to tax.

Limited Company Assets

Where a limited company purchases an asset with an element of private use the whole cost is allowable for capital allowances purposes. However, HMRC will then consider the private use element to be a taxable 'benefit in kind' which is chargeable to income tax and national insurance.

A P11D(b) will also need to be prepared and filed, resulting in additional accountancy fees.

If you were purchasing an iPad through your limited company with 50%/50% mixed use the whole asset cost would qualify for capital allowances and be an allowable deduction from taxable profits within the company.

However a taxable benefit would likely arise due to the level of personal use of the iPad. For an asset such as an iPad, the value of the benefit is calculated as 20% of the cost to the company.

The Property Tax Handbook for BRRR & BTL Investors

Example

Mary is the sole director/shareholder of ABC Quality Caravans Limited and wishes to buy a new iPad. If she were to purchase a new iPad Pro through her company the benefit would be 20% of the £1,000 as the cost of the iPad. Income tax at 20%/40%/45% and national insurance at 13.8% would then be due on the £200 benefit value. The requirement to file a P11D(b) would also arise, most likely resulting in higher accountancy fees.

To avoid a benefit in kind arising the personal use of the asset cannot be significant. If you can demonstrate that there is a genuine business purpose for providing the iPad and that any personal use is insignificant there will be no benefit in kind and no requirement to file a P11D(b).

Providing a company car where there is even the slightest element of personal use will be viewed as a taxable benefit and should generally be avoided.

Purchasing assets through a limited company where there is significant personal use is generally not advisable due to the benefit in kind implications that can arise. There are a number of exceptions to this, such as the provision of a mobile phone.

A limited company providing a director with a mobile phone, which is used for a mix of business and personal calls, would not be deemed a benefit in kind providing there is only 1 phone being provided and the phone contract is in the name of the company.

Tax tip: You can claim capital allowances on assets you owned before starting your business. For assets brought into the business you can claim capital allowances based on the market value when you first started using it for business purposes.

Flat Rate Deductions

To help simplify the record keeping process HMRC permit a number of expense deductions at a flat rate.

The Property Tax Handbook for BRRR & BTL Investors

Whether it is worth claiming the flat rate deduction or the actual amount will depend on the specific figures.

Motor expenses

If you use your private vehicle for business travel you can claim a flat rate deduction for the miles travelled. This could include checking existing properties, trips to the post office, or travelling to view a potential purchase.

Motor expenses are an area where the difference between limited companies and individuals/partnerships is significant. This first section is relevant to individuals/partnerships.

The table below outlines the rates at which a deduction is available. You should keep a detailed log of the start and end destination, number of miles, and the purpose of the journey. The deduction is given by multiplying the number of miles by the appropriate rate.

The Property Tax Handbook for BRRR & BTL Investors

The decision between actual expenses and flat rate deductions must be made when the car is first used within the business and cannot later be changed.

You cannot claim separately for the cars running cost where you also claim the flat rate deduction. Running costs include: fuel, electricity, road tax, MOTs, or repairs. Other costs incidental to the trip such as parking are allowable, providing they meet the 'wholly and exclusively' test.

Example

Pete has driven 5,500 business miles through the tax year out of a total 11,000 miles recorded on his car. Pete could choose to claim 50% (5,500 miles/ 11,000 miles) of the cars actual running costs. Alternatively, he could claim the flat rate deduction of £2,475 (45p x 5,500 miles).

Purchasing a car that has private use through a limited company will have different tax consequences. The costs of the car will always deductible within the company, either as capital allowances or a revenue expense depending on if the car is purchased outright or leased. High emission cars that are leased are subject to a restriction which results in only 85% of the total lease costs being an allowable deduction for tax purposes.

A car bought outright will qualify for capital allowances at 100%, 18% or 6% depending on its CO_2 emissions.

Electric and low emission cars will receive the 100% capital allowances rate, meaning the full cost can be deducted from taxable profits in the year of purchase.

Due to the car being available for private use, there will be a benefit in kind charge arising in a similar way to the earlier iPad example. The way in which a benefit in kind charge is calculated is by reference to its CO_2 emissions, the higher the emissions the higher the tax you pay.

HMRC rarely accept that there is no private use of a motor vehicle unless you can show it's kept within a locked car park when not used within the business, such as at the company's office car park. If you can prove there is no private use, then no benefit in kind charge will arise.

Deadlines and requirements

Each year a limited company must submit annual accounts to Companies House, these are due no later than 9 months and 1 day from the end of the companies accounting period. If there are filed late there are penalties which start at £150 for under 1 month late and increase to £1,500 where more than 6 months late.

On top of this the accounts and a Corporation Tax return must be sent to HMRC no later than 12 months from the end of the accounting period, again there are penalties for late filing.

The payment of Corporation Tax must be made before 9 months and 1 day from the end of the accounting period, where Corporation Tax is paid late HMRC charge late payment interest.

The Property Tax Handbook for BRRR & BTL Investors

Your company's accounting period by default is set to 12 months from the end of the month in which the company was incorporated.

For instance, if a company was set up on 20th November 2020, the company's accounting period would run until 30th November 2021.

You can change your accounting period to a month end of your choice, the two most common are the 31 December year end so that the company follows a calendar year, and also the 31 March year end which allows the company to follow the tax year.

The Property Tax Handbook for BRRR & BTL Investors

Profit extraction from a limited company

So, once you have built up the profits inside of a limited company you will need to extract them as tax efficiently as possible! I see it time and time again where people do not take proper advice and do things that cost them extortionate amounts in tax, such as putting through a £50,000 salary, or only repaying their directors loan account and leaving their personal allowance to go to waste.

In this section we will run through some of the more tax efficient ways to extra cash from your company.

Interest

Charging interest on a loan to a limited company is a fantastic way to extra cash from the company in a tax efficient manner. The reason for this is that interest is an allowable expense within the company (meaning you save Corporation tax at 19%) and many individuals can receive interest income either tax free or taxed at just 20%.

Where you have no other income, or only a small amount of other income such that it's under £12,500 in total, the first £5,000 of interest income that would usually be taxable is actually tax free due to a special tax band, the savings nil rate band.

Example

Jonny is a director and shareholder of his own property company, on top of this he works part time earning a salary of £12,500. He's been advised by his accountant he could save close to £1,000 just by charging interest on a loan to his own limited company.

As Jonny has a £100,000 directors loan account he could easily charge a 5% rate of interest on that loan, this would give him £5,000 per annum of income from his company.

Within the company this £5,000 would be deducted from profits meaning that tax is saved at 19% (£950). This interest income is then completely tax free for Jonny as it falls within his first £50,000 of income. This is because his £12,500 salary income all falls within the personal allowance.

When charging interest to your directors' loan account you will need to have a formal loan agreement drawn up. There is also the requirement to deduct basic rate income tax each time an interest payment is made to a director and pay this over to HMRC along with the form CT61. For this reason, we suggest only actually paying interest to directors once per year.

Jonny will then reclaim the £1,000 deducted when the interest was paid as part of his self-assessment tax return.

Tax Tip

Where you are borrowing money from investors for a period of 364 days or less there is no requirement to follow the CT61 rules and withhold interest at the basic rate.

Tax Tip

The CT61 filing and withholding of income tax only applies when paying interest to an individual, if your investor is a UK Limited company there is usually no requirement to file the CT61 and deduct basic rate tax.

There is another valuable relief available when it comes to interest income, called the personal savings allowance. In essence it allows for basic rate taxpayers to receive £1,000 of interest income tax free, with higher rate tax payers being entitled to £500. This is in addition to the savings nil rate band above if both are available.

It is quite possible for £18,500 to be receive in interest income without paying a penny in tax. This can be done by utilising the following bands:

- Personal allowance - £12,570
- Savings nil rate band - £5,000
- Personal savings allowance - £1,000

The Property Tax Handbook for BRRR & BTL Investors

- Total - £18,570

It's important to note that here the £18,570 is fully tax deductible within the company meaning Corporation tax is saved at 19%.

Interest should be charged at a commercial arm's length rate, which broadly means what someone else would charge to loan money to you under the same circumstances. We work with loan agreements for clients every day and the rates can vary with some being as high as 15%. At the moment charging interest at a rate of 10% should be more than acceptable.

Continuing with the above example, the directors loan account would need to have a balance of around £185,700 to allow for interest to be charged at 10%, giving £18,570 tax free income.

This is applicable per individual, so a husband and wife duo could easily double up here and take close to £40k tax free!

The Property Tax Handbook for BRRR & BTL Investors

Even further, when you have exhausted your tax free bands it may still pay to tax additional funds out. Where you are a basic rate taxpayer, and you have utilised the tax free allowances above, you will pay 20% Income tax on the interest received, yet in your limited company you are saving Corporation tax at 19%. This provides for an effective 1% tax rate on extracting cash from your company!

Salary

After maximising the amount of interest that can be taken it may often be best to take a small salary, not least to ensure you have a qualifying earnings period to state pension purposes.

In most cases taking a salary of more than £737 per month does not make financial sense, especially where you can charge a good amount of interest as above. A salary at this level should count for National insurance purposes, whilst still being lower enough that you do not pay National insurance at 12%, and the company does not pay Employers National insurance.

The Property Tax Handbook for BRRR & BTL Investors

The employment allowance provides relief for up to £4,000 of Employers Class 1 National Insurance contributions, these would usually be payable at 13.8% where you take a salary of more than £8,840 per year.

If you cannot charge interest, perhaps because your loan account is not large enough then taking a salary of up to £12,570 is tax efficient providing that the employment allowance is available. This is because although you personally still pay 12% National Insurance on the income above £9,568 and £12,570, the National Insurance paid is outweighed by the 19% Corporation Tax saving.

Example

Mary is a full-time property investor and is looking to extract cash from her limited company. Her directors' loan account is sitting at around £100k.

Here Mary is the only employee of the business which means that the Employment allowance will not be available, therefore we will only put through a salary of

£8,840 per year. This is completely tax free and is an expense within the company.

The salary of £8,840 will use up most of the personal allowance, leaving £3,660 available.

Interest of £9,660 is charged to the company and is taxed on Mary personally. This is taxed as follows:

- £3,660 falls within personal allowance and is tax free
- £5,000 is tax free due to the savings nil rate band
- £1,000 is tax free due to the personal savings allowance

This is similar to the earlier example where £18,570 was taken tax free, here you can see it's possible to achieve the same result by taking a mix of salary and interest.

Dividends

Where you want to take out more than the tax-free amounts from your company, after maximising the interest income it's often best to take dividends to provide the remainder of your income. Dividends are paid after a company has paid 19% Corporation tax which is why we prefer to take interest and salaries which are tax deductible.

The first £2,000 of dividends you receive each year will be tax free as a result of the dividend allowance. Amounts above this will be taxed as below:
- 7.5% where they fall in the basic rate band
- 32.5% where they fall in the higher rate band
- 38.1% for additional rate taxpayers

Example

Mike is a director and shareholder of ABC Prop Co Ltd, he has no other income and is looking to take as much as tax efficiently possible from his company. Up to £50,000 can be taken out in a tax efficient manner as follows:
- Salary of £8,840 per annum, tax free as within personal allowance
- Interest of £9,7400, tax free as uses remainder of personal allowance, the savings nil rate band and the personal savings allowance.

- Dividend income of £2,000, tax free as utilises the £2,000 dividend allowance
- Up to a further £29,500 in dividends paying only 7.5% Income tax

The personal income tax liability on circa £50,000 extracted this way would be circa £2,200. Of course, the dividends will have been subject to Corporation tax already however this would be case whether dividends are taken or not.

Dividends can only be taken where a company has sufficient retained profits, for instance where a company has made losses since its incorporation it will be unable to pay dividends. In this case the only options available to extract cash would be interest and salary.

Dividends should always be properly declared with vouchers produced confirming how much was paid and when. This is important as HMRC may wish to see this if they enquire into whether the dividend was legal and also in which year it is to be taxed.

Pension Contributions

Your limited company can make pension contributions on your behalf, these can be received tax free in the pension scheme and are usually a fully allowable expense within the company. The annual maximum you can place into a pension and still receive the tax benefits is currently £40,000. Pensions are a specialist area and it's worthwhile working with your accountant and IFA to ensure yours is being best utilised.

Repayment of Directors' Loan

Where your company owes you money this is called a directors loan, this can be repaid by the company to you at anytime tax free. For the reasons mentioned earlier it can be wise to keep a high balance on your loan account so that interest can be charged, but for those who are higher rate tax payers or already have other income using the company cash to repay the loan can be a great way to extract cash from the company.

Going overdrawn on your directors loan account should be avoided at all times as where you borrow from your own limited company and do not repay the loan with 9 months and 1, directors loan account tax at 32.5% will be due and will not be returned until the loan has been fully repaid.

The Property Tax Handbook for BRRR & BTL Investors

My Favourite Tax Deductions

Trivial benefits exemption

Using this tax efficient exemption to extract value from your company can be very valuable! The way it works is simple, the gift or benefit must:

- cost you £50 or less to provide
- it isn't cash or a cash voucher
- it isn't a reward for work or performance
- it isn't in the terms of a contract

This means as a director your company can pay for gifts such as clothes or vouchers up to the value of £50 per occasion. For directors however there is a cap of £300 per annum. It's still not bad and means 6 lots of £50 vouchers over the year. Even more this is per director so a couple could be taking out £600.

Annual Events

If your function is a recurring annual event, such as an awards dinner, a Christmas party or a summer event, and all of your employees are invited to attend and the cost of organising the event is less than £150 a head, you are not obliged to report the event to HMRC or pay any Class 1A NICs.

If your company is based across separate departments or locations, it is perfectly acceptable to hold separate functions under the same rules. The only prerequisite is that every employee is invited to attend at least one of the functions.

If the social event in question (or total of the annual cost of events) exceeds £150 per head – even by just £1, or it is not open to all employees, then these costs are not eligible to take advantage of this HMRC exemption.

Your company will be liable to pay Class 1A National Insurance on the total sum of the event costs. The costs must be reported in full to HMRC so that National

Insurance payments can be calculated and paid accordingly. It is worth noting that the £150 per head exemption applies per employee per year, not per event.

The exemption can therefore be split across multiple functions, as long as each separate event meets the other eligibility criteria.

An example of how this would work for a property business with 2 directors would be. The two directors who happen to be a married couple, happen to have a company event on 14th February, as this is an annual event open to all of the 2 employees the company card can be used to pay for a tax free dinner. As long as the £150 per annum allowance isn't exceeded this can easily be repeated another 2-3 times during the year.

Employing Your Spouse

As mentioned earlier it can be very tax efficient to take a salary to use a personal allowance that would otherwise be wasted. If your spouse helps in the business is any way a salary can be paid, providing it is commensurate to work performed. This would be a tax deductible expense for the company and likely tax free where there is no other income.

Employing Your children

Providing your child is over 13 they can work for your business just as they would a paper round. The cash will be an expense in the company providing they do undertake work in the business and are not paying paid more than then going rate. They will likely have no other income and as such should receive the income tax free.

Sell Your Assets to The Company

As we covered earlier on selling the assets which you paid for personally to the company when you start to use them for business purposes is a great tax saving tip.

The sale will have to take place at the market value at the time they started to be used for business purposes, but this will increase your directors' loan account and a company would also be able to claim capital allowances on the amount.

Tax-Free Clothing

Where you purchase clothing with the business logo on it this is an allowable expense within the business. This means that t shirts, jackets and caps which you wear whilst on work duties, as well as outside of work, can be paid for via the company and be worn by directors and employees without there being any tax charge.

FAQs

Q: What do JSM do?

A: We are accountants and tax advisers which mean we work with property investors to file all of their annual accounts and tax returns, and also provide tax advice to ensure they are being tax efficient.

Q: What makes JSM different to other accountants?

A: Not many other accountants are qualified tax advisers also, this means that you are able to benefit from expert tax advice without having the need to speak to a separate tax adviser, which would usually be charged additionally to your accounting fees.

Q: Are you accepting new clients?

A: Yes, we are currently, you can join by calling 01733 595951 or www.jsmpartners.co.uk/join

Q: How much should I be paying for accountancy fees?

A: It massively varies depending on the complexity of your business set up and the number of properties but for a landlord with 1 property in their own name our fees are £249+VAT, and for a limited company with 1 property our fees start from £89+VAT per month.

Q: What should I do to keep my accounting costs as low as possible?

A: Look to make everything as easy as possible for your accountant, including keeping transactions to a minimum, use the company bank account for all transactions, and do not set up unnecessary companies.

Q: What bookkeeping software should I use?

A: Xero or Quickbooks are both good and do the job, having used both I do prefer Xero. This is the software we recommend at JSM.

Q: Can I do my limited company accounts myself?

A: Kind of yes, you will need to find some specialist software to prepare the accounts and tax return as they

The Property Tax Handbook for BRRR & BTL Investors

need to be in a set format. We would never recommend you do your own accounts as 99/100 you will cause more damage that simply paying an accountant.

We are a leading firm of landlord, property and small business specialists with offices in London and Peterborough.

JSM.

As standard ours service includes:
- Tax strategy call when you join us
- Tax advice calls
- Accounting support calls
- Invitation to JSM events and networking
- Exclusive client only webinars
- Newsletters and exclusive resources
- Friendly and reliable service you can count on
- Fast responses no longer than 48 hours

"Josh is incredibly responsive and finds the time to talk through all my property related queries in a knowledgable and understandable way. I'm a chartered accountant myself, but I find that the property specific tax and accounting knowledge Josh has is invaluable in building my property portfolio. Highly recommended."

Neil Harding, Silverlink Property Ltd

They really understand the property world and how all the different strategies work. They really understand the best way to structure things such as deals and withdrawl of funds.

Natasha Friend, Friend Property Group Ltd

JSM have been absolutely amazing for me. I live abroad and they sorted all my personal tax. I also use JSM for my property business and they are just fantastic. Available for a chat, responsive with emails and super hard working for their clients. They are up to date with all thing tax and always sharing tips along with other amazingly useful content! An accountant for a new generation of business owners! I won't go anywhere else! Thanks Joshua and team!!

Nicola Hamilton

Printed in Great Britain
by Amazon